BOOK HOUSE
Life-Sized
BUGS

AUTHOR:
John Townsend

EDITOR:
Nick Pierce

DESIGNER:
Isobel Lundie

WILDLIFE CONSULTANT: Anja Rott

Contents

 4 Introduction

 5 Common **Bedbug**

 6 Lupin **Aphid**

 7 Asian Tiger **Mosquito**

 8 European **Earwig**

 9 Giant **Flea**

 10 **Bumblebee**

 11 Seven Spot **Ladybird**

 12 Bombardier **Beetle**

 13 Bulldog **Ant**

 14 Pacific Dampwood **Termite**

 15 Funnel-Web **Spider**

 16 Beautiful **Wood-nymph**

 17 Large Blue **Butterfly**

 18 Snowy Tree **Cricket**

 19 Mydas **Fly**

 20 Elephant Hawk-**Moth**

 21 Asian Giant **Hornet**

 22 Giant Asian **Mantis**

 23 Giant Winged **Cockroach**

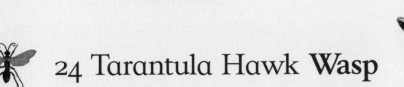 24 Tarantula Hawk **Wasp**

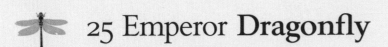 25 Emperor **Dragonfly**

 26 Stag **Beetle**

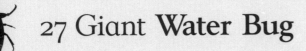 27 Giant **Water Bug**

28 Giant Prickly **Stick Insect**

29 Giant **Weta**

30 Titan **Beetle**

32 Giant Helicopter **Damselfly**

 34 Goliath **Beetle**

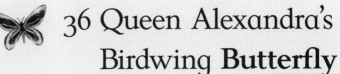 36 Queen Alexandra's Birdwing **Butterfly**

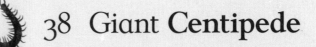 38 Giant **Centipede**

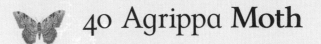 40 Agrippa **Moth**

42 Giant African **Millipede**

44 Goliath Bird-eater **Spiderlings**

46 Goliath Bird-eating **Spider**

 48-49 Glossary and Index

Introduction

This book is full of life-sized creepy-crawlies. Scientists call most of them arthropods, and some are known as bugs. A few of the arthropods here are called myriapods, which means they have lots of legs, rather than just the six legs of an insect. Spiders, with eight legs, belong to a different class altogether, called arachnids. So, whether they are true bugs, insects, spiders or myriapods, the creepy-crawlies in these pages might surprise you. They come in all shapes and sizes, but there are millions of varieties crawling, hopping or flying around us. You might want to know much more about them once you catch the BUG!

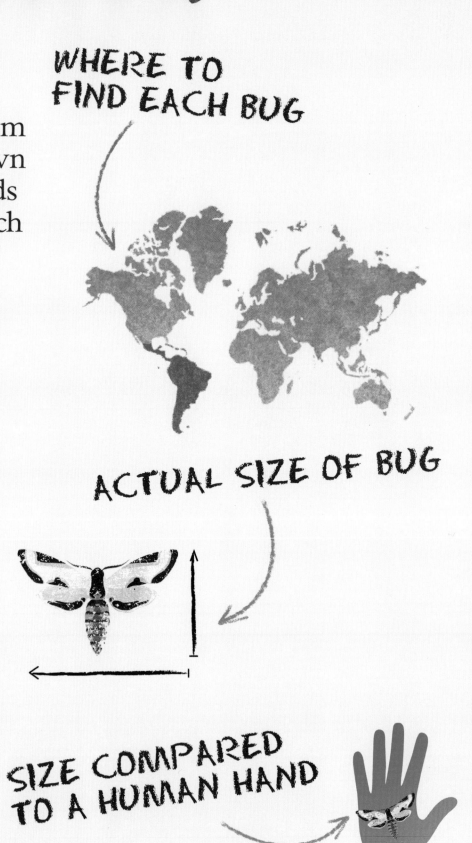

WHERE TO FIND EACH BUG

ACTUAL SIZE OF BUG

SIZE COMPARED TO A HUMAN HAND

Common Bedbug

FOUND WORLDWIDE

3 mm (about 1/4 in)

5 mm (about 1/4 in)

Bedbugs live in many places around the world, often in beds! They feed on the blood of mammals, especially humans with exposed skin for them to bite. A bedbug's saliva stops blood from clotting and the victim from feeling anything — until later when bites get red and itchy.

Bedbugs don't have wings and they can't jump. They hide in bedding and clothes, then crawl out at night, and can find a sleeping human 30 metres (about 98 feet) away.

Female bed bugs lay three or four eggs a day and up to 200 eggs in their lifetime.

MAGNIFIED!

If a bedbug feeds every ten days, it can live for 6-12 months. It can live without feeding for months. Sweet dreams!

CIMEX LECTULARIUS

Lupin Aphid

There are many types of aphid (also known as greenfly and blackfly) all around the world. In fact, aphids can come in many colours: yellow, orange, green, red, blue, purple, brown or black. They are all tiny bugs that feed by sucking sap from plants, which often causes damage to crops. That makes them a big enemy of gardeners and farmers.

Aphids are usually wingless but when food is scarce, females give birth to winged young that can fly to other areas to start new colonies.

A female can live for about 25 days and lay many eggs. Some give birth to large numbers of live young in that time.

ACTUAL APHID SIZE

6 mm (about 1/4 in)

5 mm (about 1/4 in)

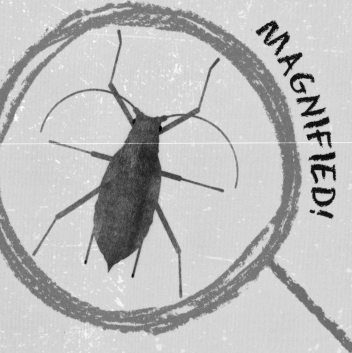

MAGNIFIED!

MACROSIPHUM ALBIFRONS

Asian Tiger Mosquito

Over 3,000 species of mosquito live around the world, near water and swamps. Some species are dangerous to humans because female mosquitoes suck blood to nourish their eggs. When some mosquitoes bite people to collect blood, they can spread malaria, yellow fever and other tropical diseases.

AEDES ALBOPICTUS

This mosquito's name comes from its black and white stripes, as well as from being an aggressive biter. It prefers human blood to other mammals.

MAGNIFIED!

13 mm (about 1/2 in)

10 mm (about 1/2 in)

Adult tiger mosquitoes live from a few days to several weeks, depending on the weather.

The Asian Tiger mosquito is a small daytime-biting insect, which spread to Europe in the 1970s. It has been spreading northwards and has even reached Britain during hot weather.

European Earwig

Earwigs use the pincers at the rear of their body, known as cerci, to protect themselves from predators. Since they are nocturnal their long feelers (antennae) help them to sense food or other earwigs. At night, they emerge to hunt tiny insects like aphids or to find plants to eat.

FOUND WORLDWIDE

FORFICULA AURICULARIA

A European earwig lives for about a year. Male earwigs often die first, when the females push them out of their burrow during the winter.

They have wings that fold up tightly on their back, but, as they are weak fliers, they mostly move around by crawling.

13 mm (about 1/2 in)

2.2 mm (about 1/10 in)

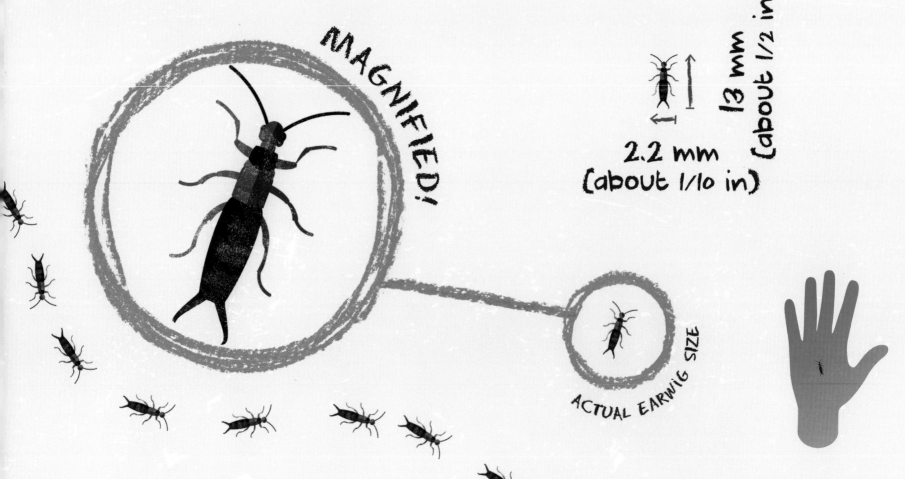

MAGNIFIED!

ACTUAL EARWIG SIZE

Giant Flea

Fleas are small flightless insects that are parasites because they feed on the blood of animals or humans. There are over 2,500 types of flea but the largest is known as the mountain beaver flea. That's because they only live on or around small north American rodents called mountain beavers.

Like all fleas, the giant flea has a mouth able to pierce skin and suck blood. Its strong hind legs allow it to leap 50 times its body length in one hop.

Generally, an adult flea only lives for two or three months but in that time a female can lay up to 5,000 eggs.

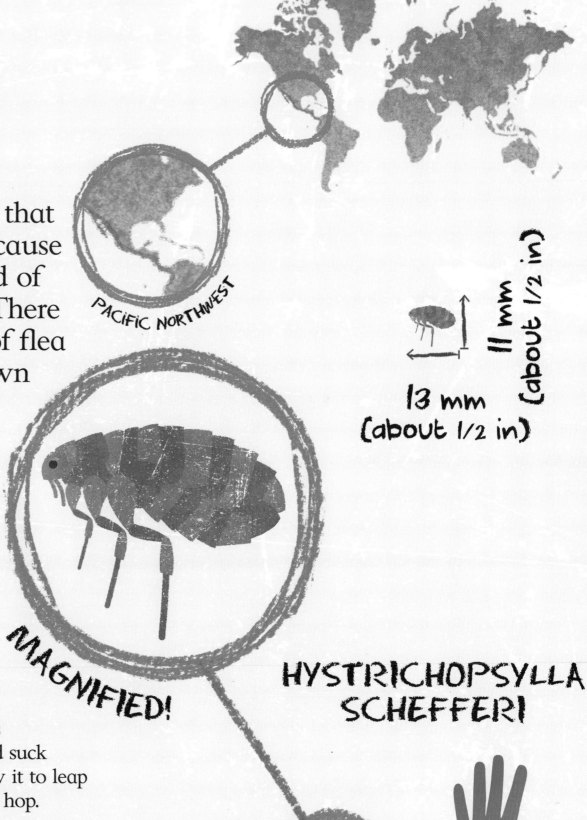

PACIFIC NORTHWEST

MAGNIFIED!

HYSTRICHOPSYLLA SCHEFFERI

ACTUAL GIANT FLEA SIZE

13 mm (about 1/2 in)

11 mm (about 1/2 in)

Bumblebee

Bumblebees are plump, hairy, yellow and black flying insects with a distinct buzz. There are over 250 species around the world, particularly in the northern hemisphere.

A bumblebee's wings move at 130-240 beats per second. This allows it to hover over flowers to collect pollen and nectar. Unlike honey bees, bumblebees can sting more than once. However, male bumblebees don't have a stinger at all, and female bumblebees aren't aggressive.

Bumblebees live in smaller groups than honey bees and don't tend to swarm. Although the queen may live up to a year, the workers only live for a few weeks.

ACTUAL BUMBLEBEE SIZE

14 mm (about 1/2 in)

15 mm (about 1/2 in)

MAGNIFIED!

BOMBUS

Seven-Spot Ladybird

Ladybirds are six-legged flying beetles, also known as ladybeetles or ladybugs. There are about 5,000 different species of ladybirds, in different colours and patterns. The most familiar in the UK is the seven-spot ladybird, which has a shiny red or orange body with three spots on each side and one in the middle.

17 mm (about 3/4 in)

18 mm (about 3/4 in)

The ladybird's bright colours warn animals not to eat it, as it oozes a foul-tasting fluid when attacked. Even so, it is hunted by some species of birds.

ACTUAL LADYBIRD SIZE

MAGNIFIED!

In its year-long life, a seven-spot ladybird can eat over 5,000 aphids.

COCCINELLA SEPTEMPUNCTATA

11

Bombardier Beetle

There are about 500 species of bombardier beetle and they all have a special way to defend themselves. They fire ammunition from their bottoms! When threatened, they eject a hot chemical explosion at would-be predators. This explosive spray can reach temperatures of 100°C, which can kill other insects and scare off larger predators. The beetle can then fly off and escape, as it has wings.

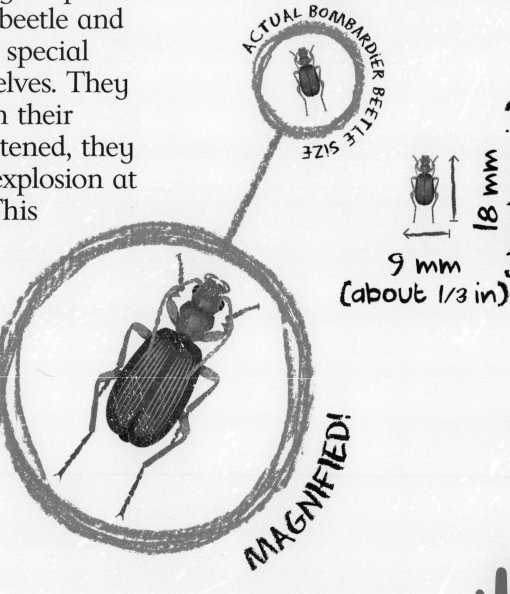

ACTUAL BOMBARDIER BEETLE SIZE

MAGNIFIED!

18 mm (about 3/4 in)

9 mm (about 1/3 in)

Bombardier beetles are carnivorous as they feed on insects and grubs.

Adult beetles usually live for several weeks.

BRACHINUS CREPITANS

Bulldog Ant

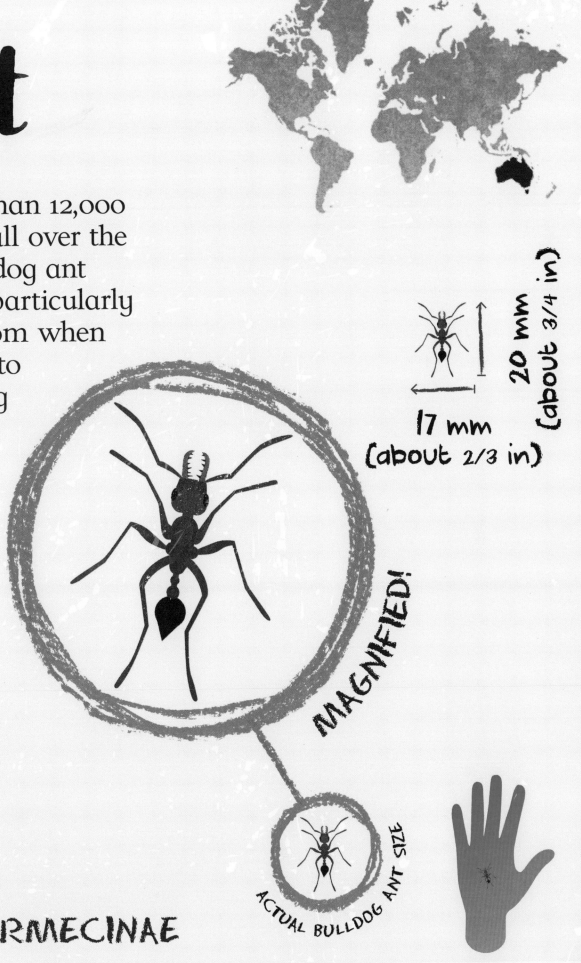

There are more than 12,000 species of ants all over the world. The bulldog ant found in Australia is particularly fierce and injects venom when it attacks. It holds on to its victim with its long mandibles and then curls its body to jab with its sting. Its sting has been known to kill some humans.

Bulldog ants eat small insects, honeydew (a sweet, sticky liquid left by some insects on leaves), seeds and fruit. The ant larvae are carnivores that eat small insects brought back to the nest by worker ants.

Bulldog ants live for eight to ten weeks from larvae to adults (about three weeks as an adult).

20 mm (about 3/4 in)

17 mm (about 2/3 in)

MAGNIFIED!

ACTUAL BULLDOG ANT SIZE

MYRMECINAE

Pacific Dampwood Termite

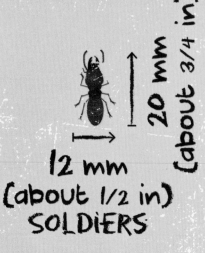

PACIFIC COAST

ACTUAL PACIFIC DAMPWOOD TERMITE SIZE

Termites are insects that eat wood. There are about 2,000 known termite species in the world and many are pests because they can chew through timber buildings, flooring and even wallpaper. Dampwood termites are normally larger than other termite species. They prefer to eat wet, mouldy wood, which is why they live in damp forests and woodlands. The Pacific dampwood termite is the largest species in the United States.

ZOOTERMOPSIS ANGUSTICOLLIS

Scientists believe some queens have a lifespan of 10-50 years.

Termites build colonies with thousands of members. The queen termite lays millions of eggs during her life.

15 mm (about 1/2 in)

9 mm (about 1/3 in)
WORKERS

20 mm (about 3/4 in)

12 mm (about 1/2 in)
SOLDIERS

25 mm (about 1 in)

14 mm (about 1/2 in)
SWARMER

Funnel-Web Spider

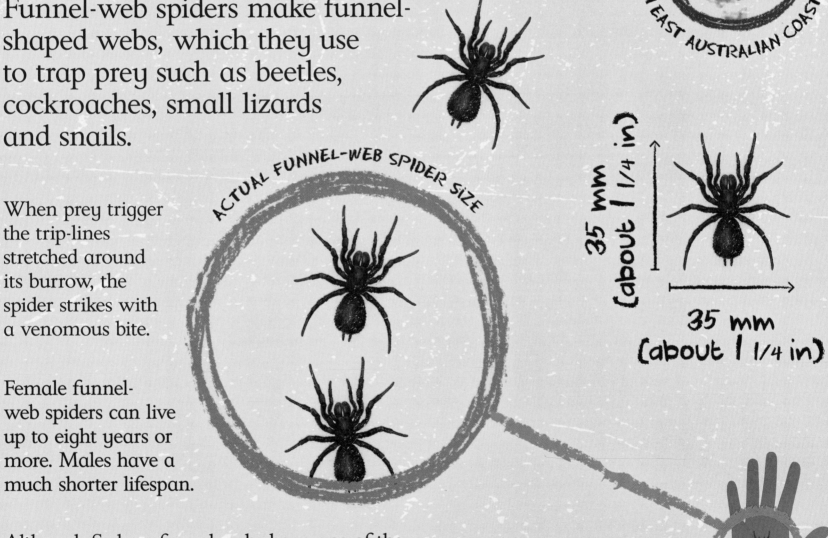

All spiders have eight legs and belong to the arachnid order, so they aren't strictly insects. Funnel-web spiders make funnel-shaped webs, which they use to trap prey such as beetles, cockroaches, small lizards and snails.

When prey trigger the trip-lines stretched around its burrow, the spider strikes with a venomous bite.

Female funnel-web spiders can live up to eight years or more. Males have a much shorter lifespan.

Although Sydney funnel-webs have one of the strongest venoms of any spider, bites to humans can now be treated so they are not always deadly. It is also a myth that these spiders jump onto people or attack them in their houses!

SOUTH EAST AUSTRALIAN COASTLINE

ACTUAL FUNNEL-WEB SPIDER SIZE

35 mm (about 1 1/4 in)

35 mm (about 1 1/4 in)

ATRACINAE

Beautiful Wood -nymph

The beautiful wood-nymph is a North American moth with a clever disguise. The best way to avoid being eaten by a predator is to look like something nasty — such as bird droppings. That's just what this moth looks like when it folds its wings and rests on a leaf or tree trunk. This camouflage keeps it safe.

Like most moths, beautiful wood-nymphs are nocturnal — which makes them different from butterflies. Whereas a butterfly's antennae are long with a bulb at the end, a moth's antennae are feathery or jagged.

29 mm (about 1 1/4 in)

45 mm (about 1 3/4 in)

Beautiful wood-nymph caterpillars feed mainly on Virginia creeper leaves.

EUDRYAS GRATA

Large Blue Butterfly

BUTTERFLY

30 mm (about 1 1/4 in)

46 mm (about 1 3/4 in)

LARVA

ACTUAL LARVA SIZE

13 mm (about 1/2 in)

5 mm (about 1/4 in)

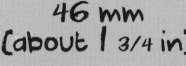

A fter becoming extinct in the British Isles in 1979, the Large Blue butterfly was reintroduced. There are now more in Britain than ever before, due to careful conservation.

The caterpillar feeds on the grubs of a red ant, on which this species depends for survival.

The caterpillar makes a honey-like fluid that red ants really like. They take the caterpillar into their nest, where it then eats their young! The ants keep drinking its 'honey' until it hibernates through the winter.

The Large Blue butterfly emerges in June and lives for up to two weeks, although often for just five days.

MAGNIFIED!

PHENGARIS ARION

Snowy Tree Cricket

There are many types of cricket (about 2,400 species of these leaping insects) around the world. The main difference between a cricket and a grasshopper is that crickets 'sing' by rubbing their wings together, while grasshoppers rub their long hind legs against their wings. Male tree crickets make chirping sounds by rubbing a scraper on one wing along a row of teeth on the opposite wing.

Crickets call more frequently when the weather gets hotter. An old belief is that if you count the number of snowy tree cricket's chirps in 14 seconds and add 40, you'll get the temperature in Fahrenheit!

Snowy tree crickets are omnivores and will eat plants, fruit, fungi, pollen and tiny insects.

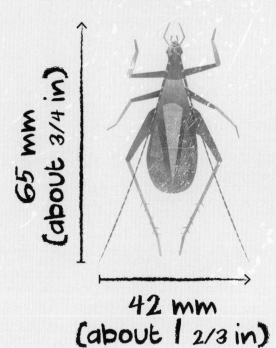

65 mm (about 3/4 in)

42 mm (about 1 2/3 in)

OECANTHUS FULTONI

Mydas Fly

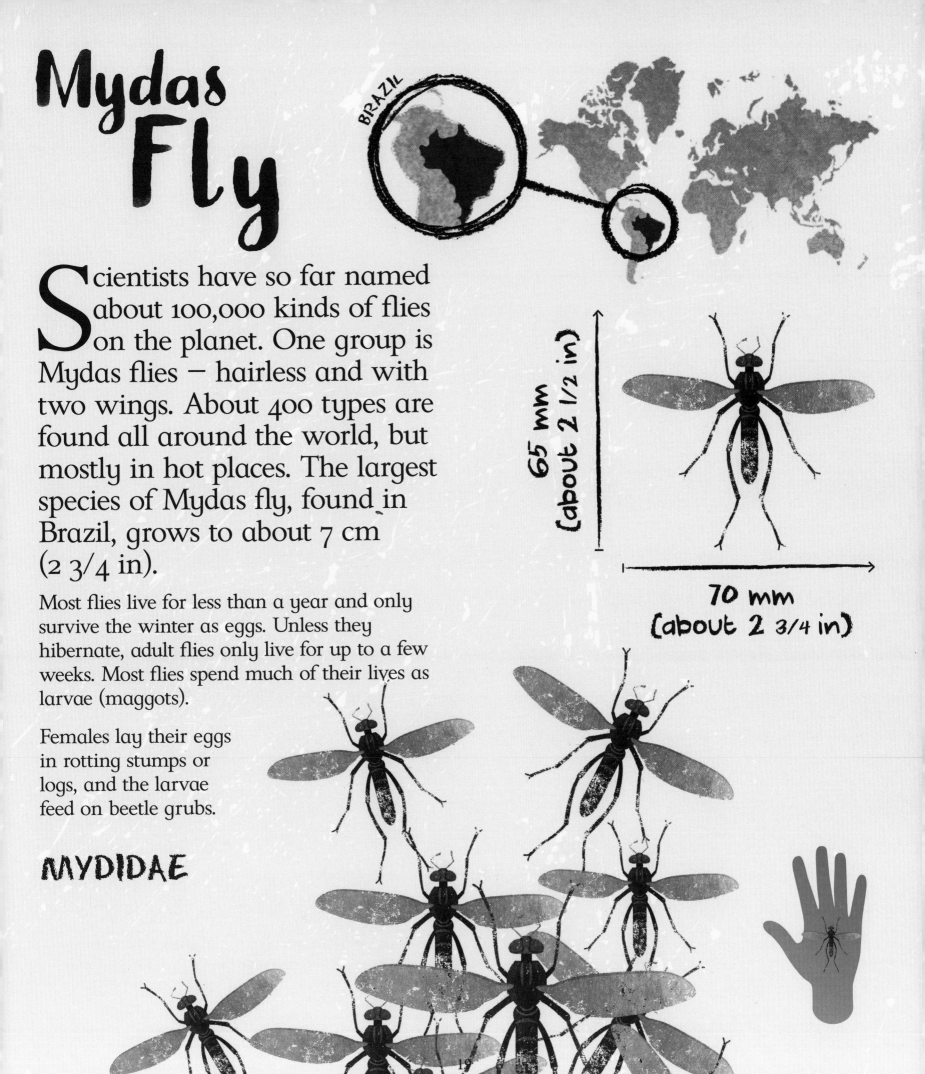

BRAZIL

Scientists have so far named about 100,000 kinds of flies on the planet. One group is Mydas flies — hairless and with two wings. About 400 types are found all around the world, but mostly in hot places. The largest species of Mydas fly, found in Brazil, grows to about 7 cm (2 3/4 in).

Most flies live for less than a year and only survive the winter as eggs. Unless they hibernate, adult flies only live for up to a few weeks. Most flies spend much of their lives as larvae (maggots).

Females lay their eggs in rotting stumps or logs, and the larvae feed on beetle grubs.

MYDIDAE

65 mm (about 2 1/2 in)

70 mm (about 2 3/4 in)

Elephant Hawk-Moth

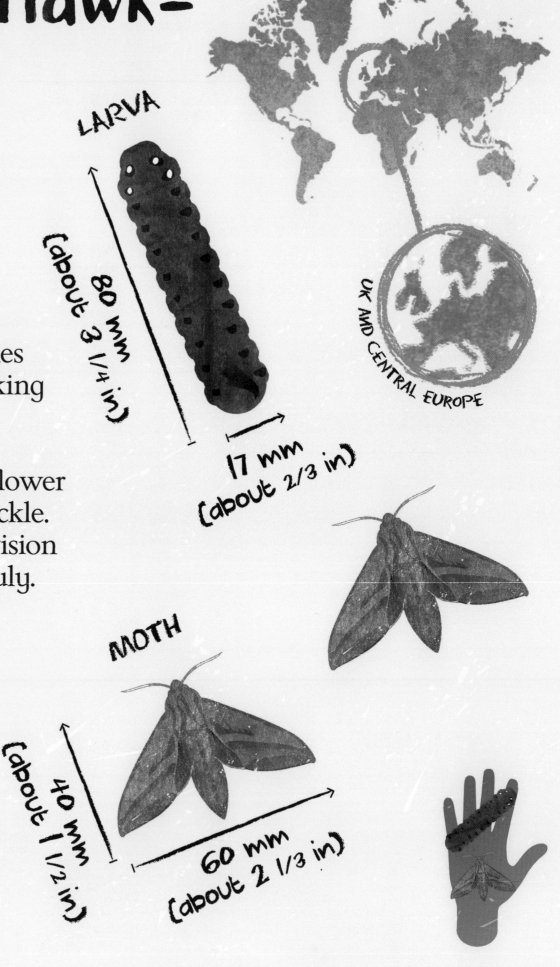

awk moths are so called because they hover and swoop like hawks. The elephant hawk-moth's name comes from the caterpillar looking a bit like an elephant's trunk. The moths are nocturnal and feed on flower nectar, such as honeysuckle. They have good night vision and live from May to July.

Like most hawk-moth larvae, the caterpillar has a so-called horn on the tip of its body. The caterpillars feed on leaves and can become prey to birds.

These moths live for about five weeks. You are more likely to see the caterpillars in late summer.

LARVA

80 mm (about 3 1/4 in)

17 mm (about 2/3 in)

UK AND CENTRAL EUROPE

MOTH

40 mm (about 1 1/2 in)

60 mm (about 2 1/3 in)

DEILEPHILA ELPENOR

Asian Giant Hornet

The Asian giant hornet is the largest species of wasp in the world. Its stinger is about 6mm (1/4 in) long. This can inject strong venom, which causes great pain to humans. These hornets prey on smaller wasps and bees, or larger insects such as the praying mantis. They often raid and destroy beehives to feed honeybee larvae to their own young.

Asian giant hornets are known for being aggressive when attacking an enemy, and can give chase for many kilometres at speeds of up to 40 kph (25 mph). They will also send out chemical signals to attract other hornets to help with the attack.

They can live for 3-5 months and have even been seen in the UK in summer.

VESPA MANDARINIA

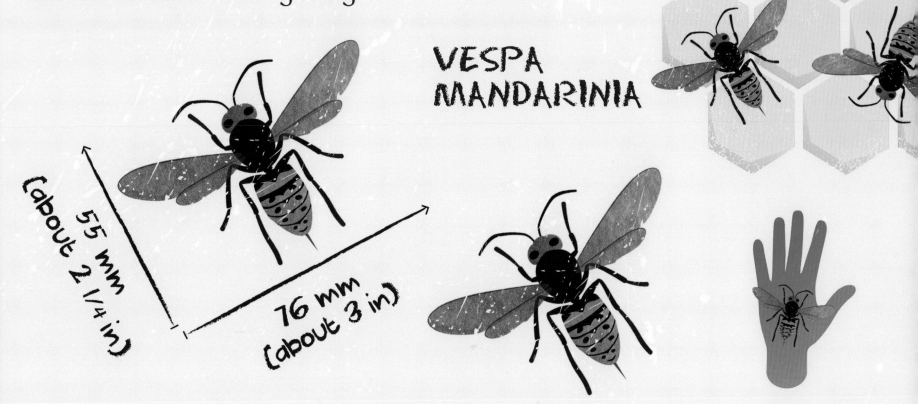

55 mm (about 2 1/4 in)

76 mm (about 3 in)

Giant Asian Mantis

There are about 2,000 species of mantis around the world. They have very sharp spines on their powerful front legs, which they use to catch their insect food. These front legs stretch up and hold together, as if the mantis is praying (they are often called praying mantises for this reason). The giant Asian mantis eats large insects in its rainforest habitat, and some larger species can even catch and eat small species of birds.

A praying mantis will also eat others of its own kind. The female will sometimes eat the male after mating to obtain important nutrients needed for her eggs.

An adult female mantis can live for about six months, although males might not be so lucky!

HIERODULA MEMBRANACEA

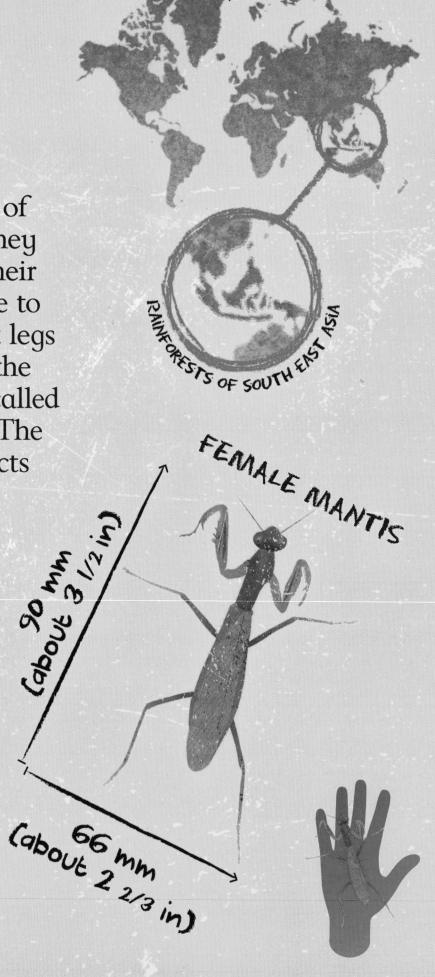

RAINFORESTS OF SOUTH EAST ASIA

FEMALE MANTIS

90 mm (about 3 1/2 in)

66 mm (about 2 2/3 in)

Giant Winged Cockroach

With over 4,000 species of cockroaches around the world, these bugs come in all sizes. The largest flying cockroach is found in South America and its wingspan can reach a massive 20 centimetres. Some are even sold as pets.

Cockroaches are sensitive to light and prefer dark, damp habitats. They do not have lungs to breathe, but instead take air in through tiny holes on the sides of their bodies. This is why a cockroach can survive for a while without its head until it starves to death.

Like all cockroaches, the giant flying species are scavengers, so they tend to eat anything, but particularly decaying plant material.

PANAMA, COLOMBIA AND PERU

97 mm (about 3 3/4 in)

45 mm (about 1 3/4 in)

MEGALOBLATTA LONGIPENNIS

Tarantula Hawk Wasp

These large wasps live wherever there are tarantula spiders to eat. But be warned – the stinger of the female wasp can be up to 7 mm (2 3/4 in) long and gives one of the most painful insect stings in the world.

The female's string paralyses a tarantula. She then drags it to her nest where she lays a single egg on the tarantula's abdomen. Once the egg hatches, the larva crawls inside to feed on the spider. After about three weeks, an adult wasp emerges to feed on flower nectar for its two-month lifespan.

PEPSINI

94 mm (about 3 2/3 in)

100 mm (about 4 in)

Emperor Dragonfly

Dragonflies and their smaller cousins, damselflies, spend most of their lives as larvae and nymphs. They hatch from eggs under water and feed on water insects, tiny fish and tadpoles. After about a year, they emerge as stunning flying adult dragonflies but only live for about ten days. They often fly high into the sky to catch prey, such as mosquitoes and butterflies.

ANAX IMPERATOR

The emperor dragonfly is one of Europe's largest dragonflies. The male is a shimmering green with blue abdomen and blue eyes. He will fight other dragonflies to the death.

The female is mostly green and lays her eggs in floating pondweed.

78 mm (about 3 in)

106 mm (about 4 1/4 in)

Stag Beetle

The Stag Beetle is the UK's largest beetle and it is found in south-east England in woodlands and gardens. The larvae live in old trees and rotting wood, taking up to six years to develop into an adult. The adults emerge in May and die in August, once they have laid their eggs in rotting wood.

Males fly in search of a mate, displaying large antler-like jaws to impress females and to fight other males (just like stags do).

These magnificent beetles are harmless to people and are now endangered by the loss of their habitats.

LUCANUS CERVUS

UK AND WESTERN EUROPE

MALE STAG BEETLE

75 mm (about 3 in)

75 mm (about 3 in)

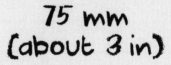

110 mm (about 4 1/4 in)

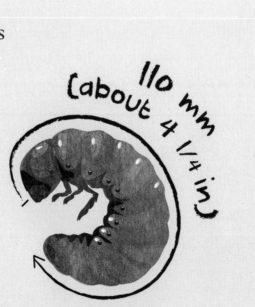

STAG BEETLE LARVA

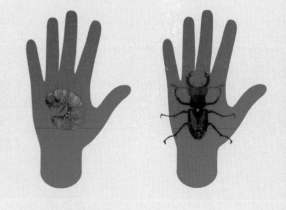

Giant Water Bug

The largest bug that lives in water is the giant water bug of Venezuela and Brazil. This swimming insect is a carnivore. It kills other insects and small fish by stabbing them with its beak-like mouth and injecting venom. Its bite is sometimes used in self-defence against humans. It is one of the most painful insect bites — its effects last for hours.

115 mm (about 4 1/2 in)

95 mm (about 3 3/4 in)

Giant water bugs, like all 'true bugs', have specialised mouth parts for piercing and sucking. They can breathe underwater using the air bubbles they trap on their body.

The Giant Water Bug takes 1-2 months to grow from nymph to adult and then lives for about one year.

LETHOCERUS MAXIMUS

Giant Prickly Stick Insect

The giant prickly stick insect (also known as Macleay's Spectre) is a large stick insect with amazing camouflage. In fact, it looks more like a cactus than a stick! Its body is covered in small spines that protect it and also make it look more like a small branch. Predators are unlikely to see it when it's in a Eucalyptus tree nibbling at leaves.

Their average lifespan is 6-9 months for males and 9-18 months for females

EXTATOSOMA TIARATUM

QUEENSLAND, NEW SOUTH WALES AND NEW GUINEA

150 mm (about 6 in)

82 mm (about 3 1/4 in)

Males have long wings so they can fly, while the bulkier females have only small wings.

Giant Weta

DEINACRIDA

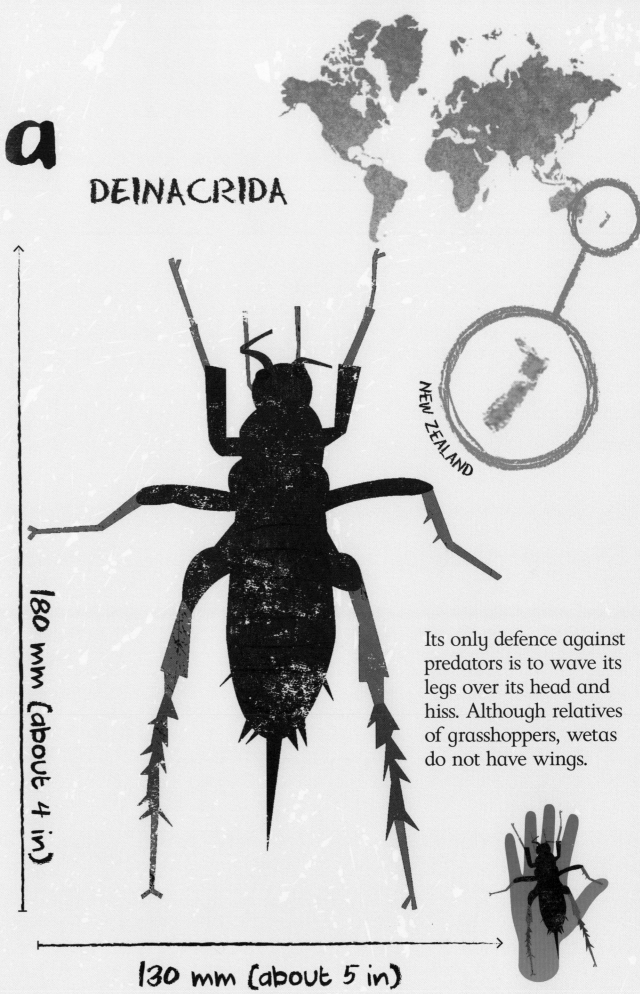

NEW ZEALAND

The giant weta is one of the biggest insects on Earth and can weigh more than a mouse. Its full name in Greek means 'terrible grasshopper' but it isn't aggressive and eats mainly plants. Birds, rats and reptiles prey on wetas, so now they only remain on small islands off the coast of New Zealand.

180 mm (about 4 in)

Its only defence against predators is to wave its legs over its head and hiss. Although relatives of grasshoppers, wetas do not have wings.

It takes most of the giant weta's two-year lifespan to reach full adult size.

130 mm (about 5 in)

Titan Beetle

The Amazon rainforest is home to many large beetles, but the biggest of all is the titan beetle. Although these insects look scary, they're not aggressive. Even so, its jaws (called mandibles) can easily snap a pencil in half and give you a nasty nip. When threatened by a predator, the beetle will hiss.

TITANUS GIGANTEUS

180 mm (about 7 in)

LARVA

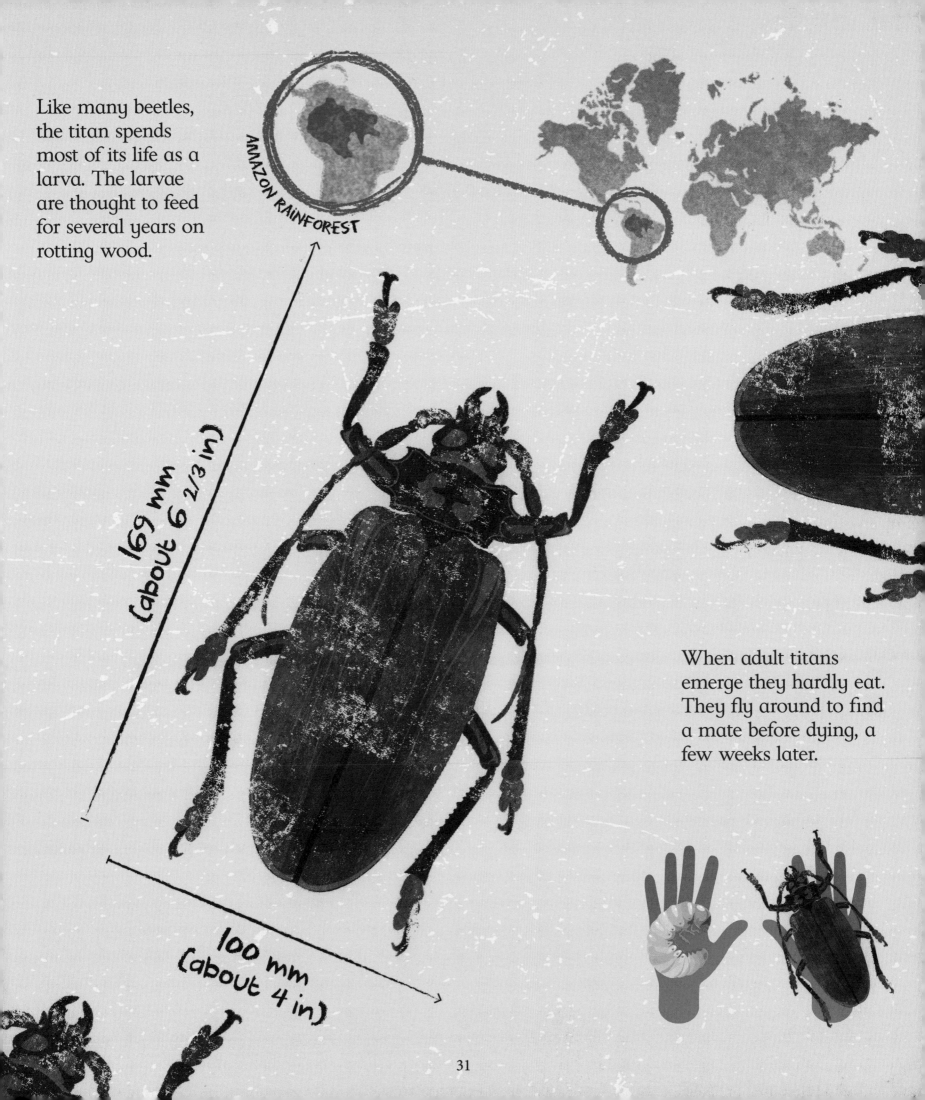

Like many beetles, the titan spends most of its life as a larva. The larvae are thought to feed for several years on rotting wood.

AMAZON RAINFOREST

169 mm (about 6 2/3 in)

100 mm (about 4 in)

When adult titans emerge they hardly eat. They fly around to find a mate before dying, a few weeks later.

Giant Helicopter Damselfly

The giant helicopter damselfly is the largest damselfly in the world and a hungry predator in both water and sky. The young (nymphs) feed on mosquito larvae, tadpoles and other nymphs, while adults feed on forest spiders. Females lay their eggs in water-filled holes in trees in the hot and humid rainforests of Central and South America.

Nymphs change into stunning, gigantic damselflies with stick-like bodies and shimmering wings with metallic-blue bands.

Adults can live for several weeks, and sometimes up to seven months.

GIANT HELICOPTER DAMSELFLY NYMPH

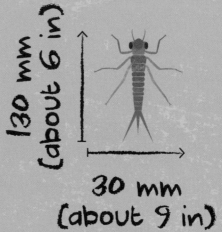

130 mm (about 6 in)

30 mm (about 9 in)

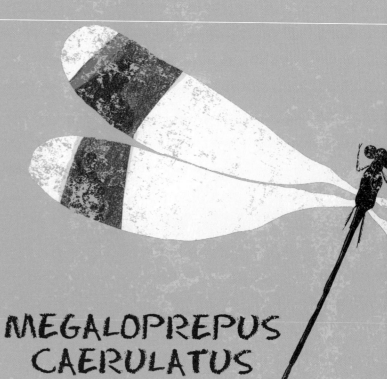

MEGALOPREPUS CAERULATUS

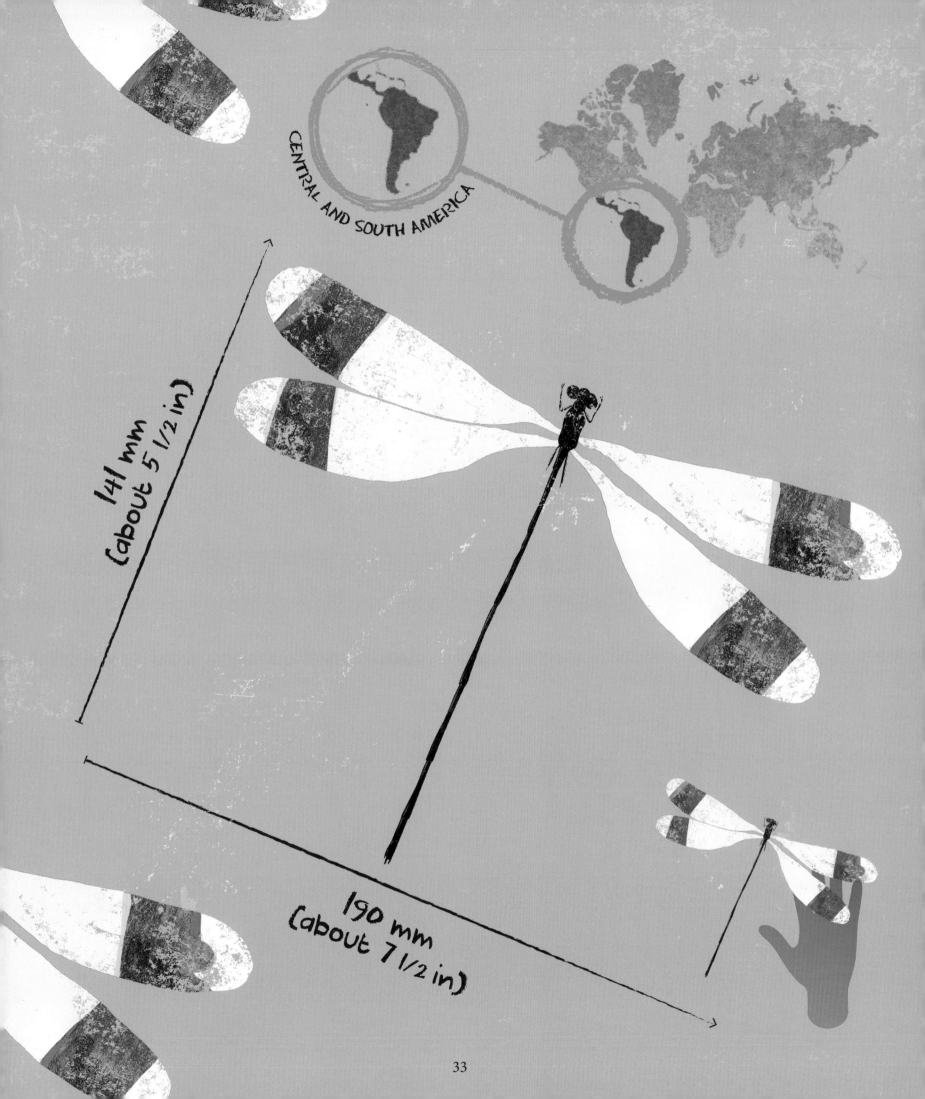

CENTRAL AND SOUTH AMERICA

141 mm
(about 5 1/2 in)

190 mm
(about 7 1/2 in)

Goliath Beetle

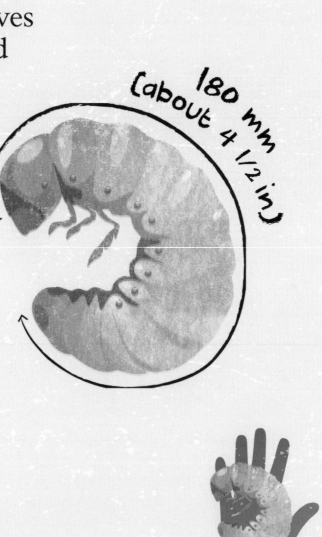

Goliath beetles are big, but their larvae are bigger and heavier. This greedy grub can weigh over 115 grams (about twice as heavy as a tennis ball). It lives in the soil and feeds on dead leaves and plants.

An adult goliath beetle is very strong. It can lift 850 times its own body weight. They live for about three months.

GOLIATHUS

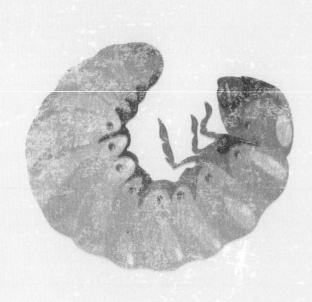

180 mm
(about 4 1/2 in)

152 mm
(about 6 in)

RAINFORESTS OF AFRICA

After hatching from an egg, the larva eats hungrily for a few months, growing very plump. An adult beetle finally emerges to fly off and mate.

227 mm (about 9 in)

Queen Alexandra's Birdwing Butterfly

The caterpillar moults six times as it grows, before emerging from a chrysalis as an enormous butterfly.

The Queen Alexandra's birdwing is famous for being the largest butterfly in the world. The female is bigger than the male, but the male is much more brightly coloured. It is now an endangered species because of the cutting down of rainforests where it lives. As a caterpillar, it is black with red spikes and a yellow stripe. It feeds on poisonous vines that make it poisonous to eat, so its bright colours warn predators to keep away. In the three months of its adult life it feeds on flower nectar.

90 mm (about 3 1/2 in)

ORNITHOPTERA ALEXANDRAE

EAST PAPUA NEW GUINEA

280 mm
(about 11 in)

Giant Centipede

The largest centipede in the world, it is also known as the Peruvian giant yellow-leg centipede.
It has a pair of mandibles (called forcipules) that can bite prey and deliver venom to victims such as mice, lizards, frogs and even large tarantula spiders. They can hang from cave roofs to catch flying birds and bats.

SCOLOPENDRA
GIGANTEA

300 mm
(about 11 3/4 in)

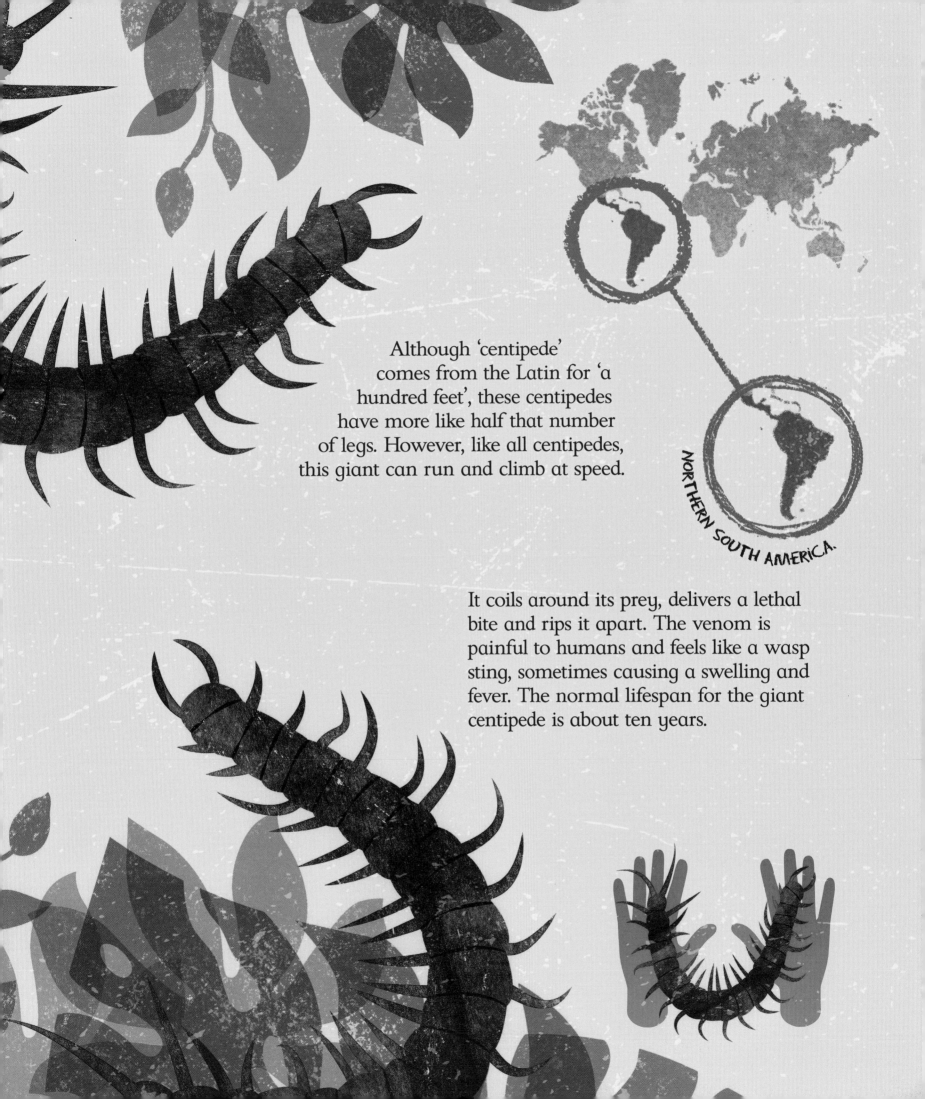

Although 'centipede' comes from the Latin for 'a hundred feet', these centipedes have more like half that number of legs. However, like all centipedes, this giant can run and climb at speed.

NORTHERN SOUTH AMERICA.

It coils around its prey, delivers a lethal bite and rips it apart. The venom is painful to humans and feels like a wasp sting, sometimes causing a swelling and fever. The normal lifespan for the giant centipede is about ten years.

Agrippa Moth

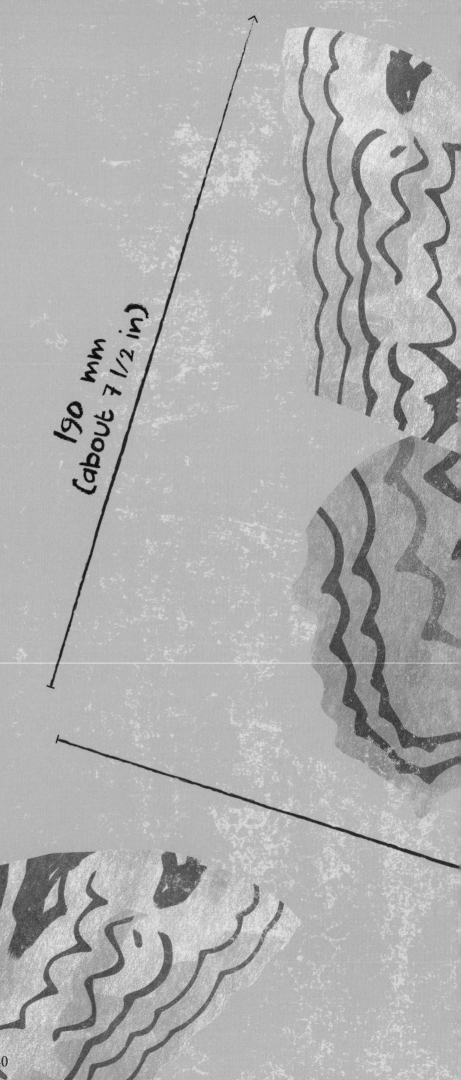

The moth with the biggest wingspan from tip to tip is the Agrippa Moth, also known as the Ghost Moth and the White Witch. Being so large, this moth is often mistaken for a bat or bird fluttering through the trees at night. When it lands on a tree trunk, it disappears because its gold and brown patterns make excellent camouflage. Any predator searching for a particularly big moth-meal would have difficulty finding it, especially in the dark.

190 mm (about 7 1/2 in)

Like most moths, the Agrippa Moth lives for only about a week or two after emerging from its chrysalis. In that time, it hardly feeds. It looks for a mate, lays its eggs and dies shortly afterwards.

THYSANIA AGRIPPINA

310 mm
(about 12 1/4 in)

Giant African Millipede

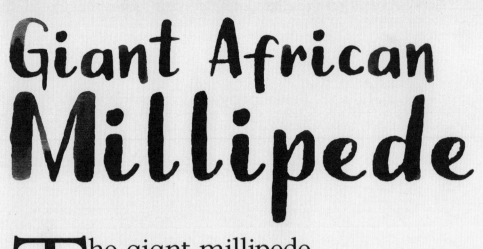

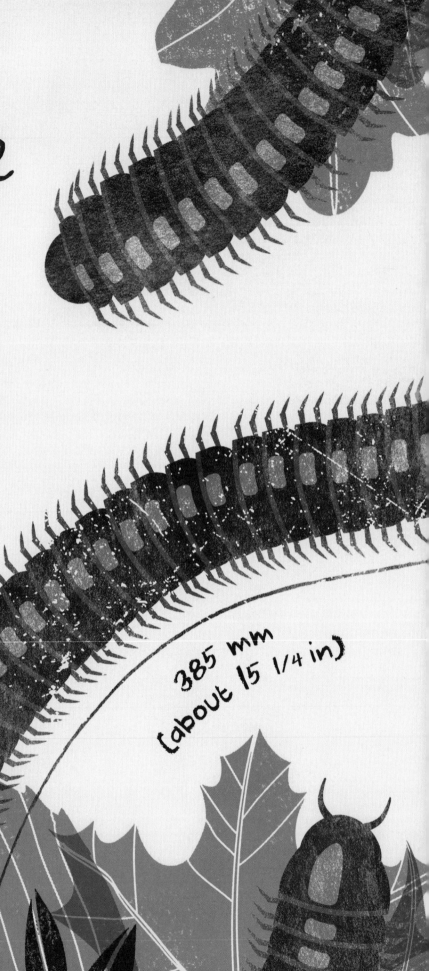

T he giant millipede is the largest of the 10,000 species of millipede in the world. It has about 250 legs, although the number changes each time it moults.

These millipedes are nocturnal and burrow into the forest floor where they feed on dead and decaying plants.

Giant millipedes are popular pets as they don't have a venomous bite like centipedes. They usually live for five to seven years.

385 mm
(about 15 1/4 in)

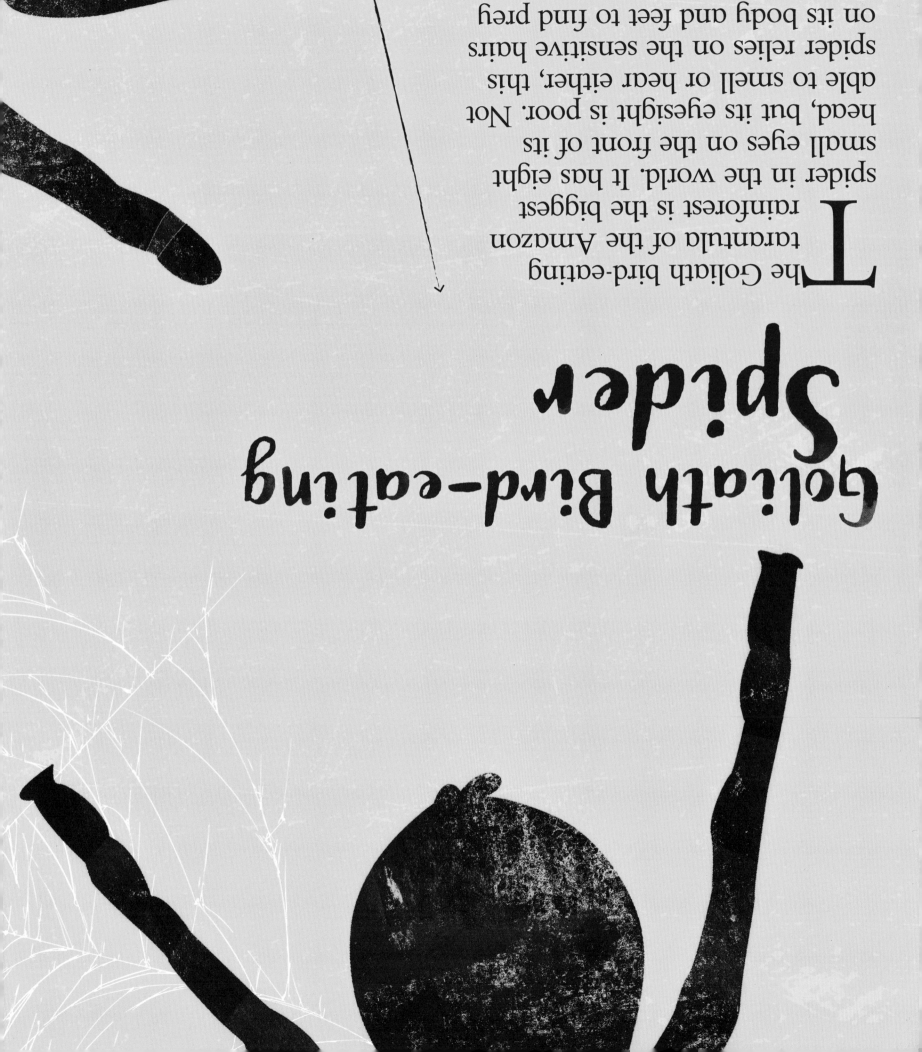

Goliath Bird-eating Spider

The Goliath bird-eating tarantula of the Amazon rainforest is the biggest spider in the world. It has eight small eyes on the front of its head, but its eyesight is poor. Not able to smell or hear either, this spider relies on the sensitive hairs on its body and feet to find prey and to deal with predators.

Goliath Birdeater
Spiderlings

Baby tarantula spiders (spiderlings) hatch from their silky egg sacs. Their eight legs, eight eyes and mini-fangs are already developed. Goliath bird-eating spiderlings are large enough to scuttle off in search of insects as soon as they leave the nest.

A mother goliath bird-eating spider lays from 50 to 150 eggs in a silk sac inside a burrow, which she guards fiercely. After a month or two, the spiderlings hatch and stay inside the burrow just until their first moult. They then scamper off to fend for themselves.

A NEST OF SPIDERLINGS

They will curl into a ball if disturbed and release an unpleasant liquid. This defence mechanism helps to protect them from predators in the African rainforest, such as birds, small mammals, frogs and snakes.

EAST AFRICA

ARCHISPIROSTREPTUS GIGAS

Despite their name, Goliath bird-eating spiders don't often eat birds, except maybe the occasional small humming bird. Their main prey are mice, lizards, frogs, bats and insects. Although their fangs are 2.5 centimetres long, their bite only injects a mild venom to humans, causing discomfort for a few hours. Some people who live in the Amazon rainforest eat these spiders by roasting them in banana leaves.

THERAPHOSA BLONDI

310mm (about 12 1/2 in)

300 mm
(about 12 1/4 in)

Glossary

Abdomen
The hind part of an insect's body, containing the stomach.

Antenna (plural: antennae)
The feelers on an insect's head.

Arachnid
Arthropods with eight legs, such as spiders.

Arthropod
An animal with no spine, a hard exoskeleton (outer-skin), jointed legs and a body divided into different parts.

Cerci
Jointed parts of an insect that stick out from the back end of its body.

Chrysalis
The pupa stage when a larva develops into an adult inside a cocoon shell.

Larva (plural: larvae)
Young of an arthropod – very different from the adult.

Mandible
Mouthparts of some insects that form their biting organs.

Myriapod
A special type of arthropod, including millipedes and centipedes.

Nocturnal
Active at night.

Nymph
The in-between stage from larva to adult.

Omnivore
A plant-eater that also eats meat.

Parasite
An animal or plant that lives in or on another living thing.

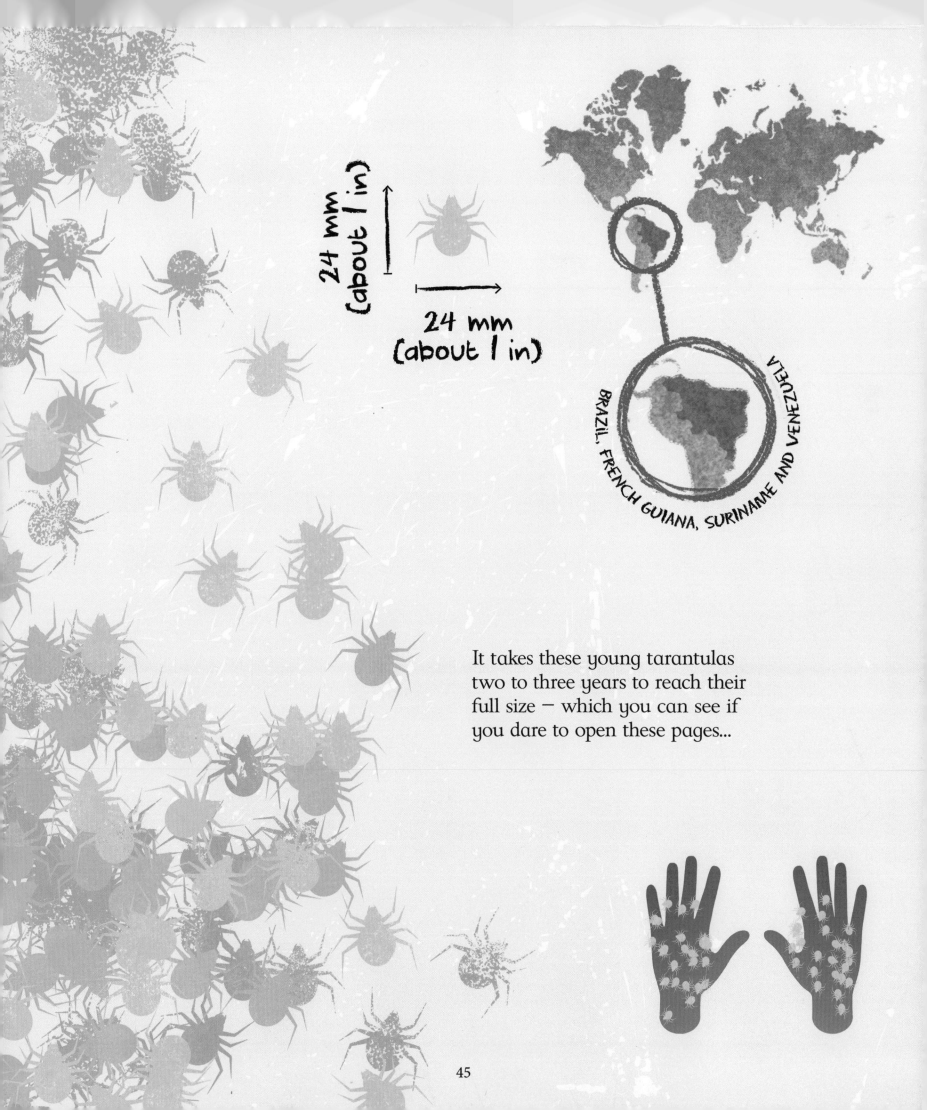

24 mm (about 1 in)

24 mm (about 1 in)

BRAZIL, FRENCH GUIANA, SURINAME AND VENEZUELA

It takes these young tarantulas two to three years to reach their full size — which you can see if you dare to open these pages...

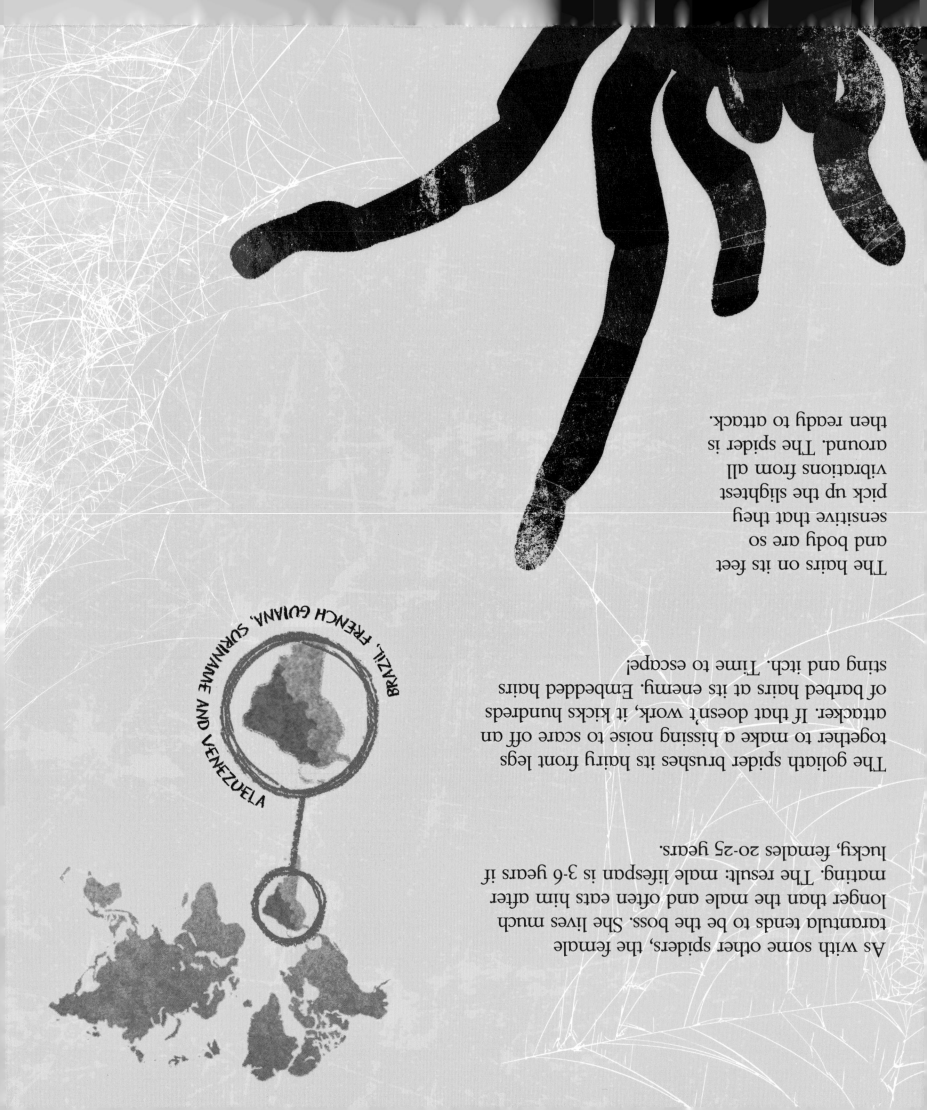

The hairs on its feet and body are so sensitive that they pick up the slightest vibrations from all around. The spider is then ready to attack.

The goliath spider brushes its hairy front legs together to make a hissing noise to scare off an attacker. If that doesn't work, it kicks hundreds of barbed hairs at its enemy. Embedded hairs sting and itch. Time to escape!

As with some other spiders, the female tarantula tends to be the boss. She lives much longer than the male and often eats him after mating. The result: male lifespan is 3-6 years if lucky, females 20-25 years.

BRAZIL, FRENCH GUIANA, SURINAME AND VENEZUELA

Index

A

antenna 8, 16
aphid 6, 8, 11

B

bedbug 5
beetle 11, 12, 15, 19, 26, 30, 31, 34, 35
bug 4, 5, 6, 11, 23, 27
butterfly 16, 17, 36, 37

C

caterpillar 16, 17, 20, 36
centipede 38, 39, 42
cerci 8
chrysalis 36, 41

D

damselfly 32, 33
dragonfly 25

E

earwig 8
eggs 5, 6, 7, 9, 14, 19, 25, 26, 32, 41, 44

F

flea 9
fly 6, 16, 17, 19, 23, 24, 25, 26, 28, 31, 32, 33, 34, 36, 37

H

hiss 29, 30, 47

L

larva 13, 17, 19, 20, 21, 24, 25, 26, 30, 31, 32, 34, 35

M

mandible 13, 30
millipede 42, 43
mosquito 7, 25, 32
moth 16, 20, 40, 41
myriapod 4

N

nocturnal 8, 16, 20, 42
nymph 16, 25, 27, 32

O

omnivore 18

P

parasite 9

R

rainforest 30, 32, 36, 46

S

spider 4, 15, 24, 32, 38, 44, 46, 47
sting 10, 13, 21, 24, 27, 39, 47

T

tarantula 24, 38, 44, 45, 46, 47

V

venom 13, 15, 21, 27, 38, 39, 42, 46

W

weta 29

Author:

John Townsend worked as a secondary school teacher before becoming a full time writer of children's books and a writer-in-residence in a primary school tree-house. He specialises in fun, exciting information books for reluctant readers, as well as fast-paced fiction, reading schemes and 'fiction with facts' books. He visits schools around the country to encourage excitement in all aspects of reading and writing. He has recently written 12 plays based on Salariya's *You Wouldn't Want To Be* series that have been uploaded to the company's new website for use in classrooms.

Wildlife consultant:

Anja Rott is an entomologist (studying insects) lecturing in Ecology at the University of Brighton. Her principle areas of research are centred on questions in the field of ecological entomology, especially population dynamics of herbivorous insects, pollination ecology (biodiversity & conservation) and dung beetle communities.

Series creator:

David Salariya was born in Dundee, Scotland. He has illustrated a wide range of books and has created and designed many new series for publishers in the UK and overseas. David established The Salariya Book Company in 1989. He lives in Brighton, England, with his wife, illustrator Shirley Willis, and their son, Jonathan.

Editor:

Nick Pierce

Designer:

Isobel Lundie

Published in Great Britain in MMXIX by
Book House, an imprint of
The Salariya Book Company Ltd
25 Marlborough Place, Brighton BN1 1UB
www.salariya.com

ISBN: 978-1-912537-74-7

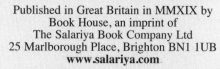

1 3 5 7 9 8 6 4 2

A CIP catalogue record for this book is available from the British Library.

Printed and bound in China.
Printed on paper from sustainable sources.

Visit
www.salariya.com
for our online catalogue and
free fun stuff.

PAPER FROM
SUSTAINABLE FORESTS